THE FIRST BOOK OF THE
SUPREME COURT

by HAROLD COY

Pictures by HELEN BORTEN

FRANKLIN WATTS
NEW YORK

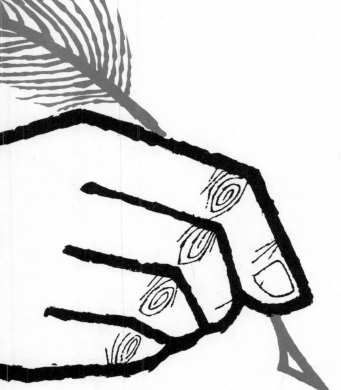

The author wishes to thank Banning
E. Whittington, Press Officer, Supreme
Court of the United States, for his help-
ful suggestions concerning the text of
this book.

8 9 10

Library of Congress Catalog Card Number: 58-6507
© Copyright 1958 by Franklin Watts, Inc.
Printed in the United States of America by the Polygraphic Company of America

Contents

How Would You Decide This Case?

Mrs. Julia V. Miller adored the red cedars at her country home in Virginia. The saplings made nice Christmas trees. When the bigger trees were thinned out, she sold the logs for fence posts. Best of all, the grove was ornamental. It lent distinction to her place.

The applegrowers of the neighborhood did not share Mrs. Miller's enthusiasm for red cedars. Every spring breeze carried the spores of the cedar rust disease from her grove into their orchards.

It's funny about cedar rust. It rocks along quietly in the cedar boughs, seemingly content to live and let live. Once it gets among apples, though, it cuts loose, sparing neither leaves nor fruit. But it can't keep going at all without that quiet period on the cedars.

The applegrowers grew long faces, watching their fine Albemarle Pippins turn rust-spotted and knobby. They showered complaints on State Entomologist W. J. Schoene. After investigating, he told Mrs. Miller it was too bad, but she would have to cut down the cedar grove.

1

"It's the law," he explained, going on to tell her about Virginia's Cedar Rust Act for the protection of applegrowers. Cut down the cedars, and the rust goes too.

Mrs. Miller protested, "I am a cedargrower. I have as much right to my property as an applegrower has to his." Her mind made up, she hired a lawyer and fought for her cedars all through the state courts. She lost. But there was still a chance. Her lawyer went to the highest court in the land, the Supreme Court of the United States. Her case was known as *Miller* v. *Schoene* (Miller *versus*, or against, Schoene).

Mrs. Miller's lawyer claimed that the Virginia law was contrary to the Constitution of the United States. It took away one person's property to help another person. Imagine how the value of Mrs. Miller's property would go down without her beautiful trees! Applegrowers had no right to shift their misfortunes to cedargrowers, Mrs. Miller's lawyer said.

Mr. Schoene's lawyer praised Virginia's famous apples. Orchards worth millions of dollars would die if cedars remained. Thousands of jobs would melt away. No one had a right to injure the state's prosperity, he claimed.

How would you decide this case? Would you tell Mrs. Miller to cut down her trees, or would you tell Mr. Schoene to let them alone?

Here's what the Supreme Court decided. Something had to go, apples or cedars; the state must make a choice. In such circumstances, said the Court, the state had the power to decide upon the destruction of one class of property in order to save another which, in the judgment of the legislature, was of greater value to the public.

That was the end of Mrs. Miller's cedars. The law was on the side of Mr. Schoene and the apples.

2

"It's the Law of the Land"

The case of the cedars versus the apples brings out the following points: A state may pass reasonable laws to protect the safety and health of its people. But a state law which conflicts with the United States Constitution must give way. The Constitution, for example, safeguards a person's property rights. At the same time, the neighbors have a right to be safe from harm. One right must sometimes be balanced against another.

The Supreme Court has to decide these matters. It holds the delicate balance between freedom and authority . . . between private property and public welfare . . . between the states and the nation. When the Supreme Court speaks, it has the final say as to what the law is.

What Is the Supreme Court?

The Constitution entrusts the "**judicial power** of the United States" to the Supreme Court and to lower courts established by Congress. Judicial power is the court's power to decide cases under the laws. This power ranks beside Congress' **legislative,** or lawmaking, **power** and the President's **executive power** to put the laws into effect.

The **judiciary** is the branch of the government that holds judicial power. It is one of the three separate and equal branches of the government established by the Constitution, and it is headed by the Supreme Court in Washington, D. C., the nation's capital. This Court

4

consists of the Chief Justice of the United States and eight Associate Justices, appointed, when a vacancy occurs, by the President then in office. All over the nation there are lesser federal courts, and state courts.

When the Founding Fathers had agreed on some ground rules for the nation, they put them into a written Constitution. Smarting from wrongs done by the British king's officials, the Fathers set up a **government of limited powers.** They gave certain powers to the federal government and left others to the states. They made lists of the things Congress, the President, and the courts can do. Beside the "cans" they put in "can'ts" — certain things the federal government can't do, others that state governments can't do, and some that can't be done by any government.

The "cans and can'ts" of the Constitution aren't ordinary laws that can be wiped off the books by a simple vote of our representatives. Changing the Constitution is a hard, slow process. It was planned that way on purpose, so that changes, which are of great importance, will be made only after plenty of discussion.

Under the Constitution neither Congress nor a state legislature could pass a law saying, "Joe Doakes is a rascal and shall be hanged" or "What Doakes did yesterday was a crime." The first law would be a **bill of attainder,** finding Joe guilty without trial; the second would be an **ex post facto law,** which punishes a person for something that wasn't a crime when he did it.

But suppose such a law is passed anyway. Joe is arrested under it and brought to trial. The judge studies the new law carefully, then looks into the Constitution and reads that no such law may be passed. Now he must choose between two laws: the new one and the Constitution. Which applies to Joe? No doubt the judge will rule that the Constitution is the higher law, and therefore the lesser law is **uncon-**

5

stitutional and of no effect. If the judge doesn't rule this way, Joe's lawyer will surely **appeal** the case (take it for review) to a higher court.

The process of comparing a law with a higher law in order to reach a decision is called **judicial review.** Article VI of the Constitution declares the **supreme law of the land** to be:

"This Constitution,

The laws of the United States made in pursuance thereof,

All treaties made under the authority of the United States."

Thus a federal law *not* made in pursuance of the Constitution is unconstitutional. But a law that Congress has a constitutional right to pass is supreme over a conflicting state law. And so are treaties and the Constitution itself.

Court judges in every state are duty bound to give the right-of-way to the "supreme law of the land": the federal constitution, laws made under it, and United States treaties. State laws that conflict with the supreme law must yield. So must any federal laws not in harmony with the Constitution.

Most cases that involve contradictory laws are not as clear as that of Joe Doakes. Numerous court decisions, no matter which way they go, are appealed. Many reach the Supreme Court for judicial review, and that court has the final say.

How Cases Reach the Court

"I'll win this case if I have to take it all the way to the Supreme Court!"

So says many a man, on starting a lawsuit. But he's not likely to get that far. Not many over a couple of hundred cases reach the Supreme Court each year. All the others run their course in the lower courts.

Local **trial courts** in cities, towns, and county seats try most criminal cases and disputes between private persons. These trial courts are part of the network of state courts. **Appellate courts,** including state supreme courts, hear appeals from trial courts.

Cases may be carried from a state court to the Supreme Court of the United States only if a **federal question** arises. A federal question is one that hinges on the meaning of the Constitution or of a federal law or a treaty. For instance, there may be a seeming conflict between a state and a federal law. Or perhaps someone claims that a state court has denied him a constitutional right. Ordinarily a federal question must be passed on by the highest state court before the Supreme Court will consider it.

Certain other cases begin in the federal courts. **United States District Courts** try those cases involving the application of federal laws to patents, bankruptcy, naturalization, maritime affairs, and such crimes as mail theft or counterfeiting. In addition, any suit between citizens of different states — like one for injuries suffered in an automobile collision — may be heard in a District Court if at least $3,000 is at stake. There are one or more District Courts in every state and territory, besides a Customs Court in New York and a Court of Claims and a Court of Customs and Patent Appeals in Washington, D. C. In each of eleven **circuits,** or regions, covering the whole of the United States and

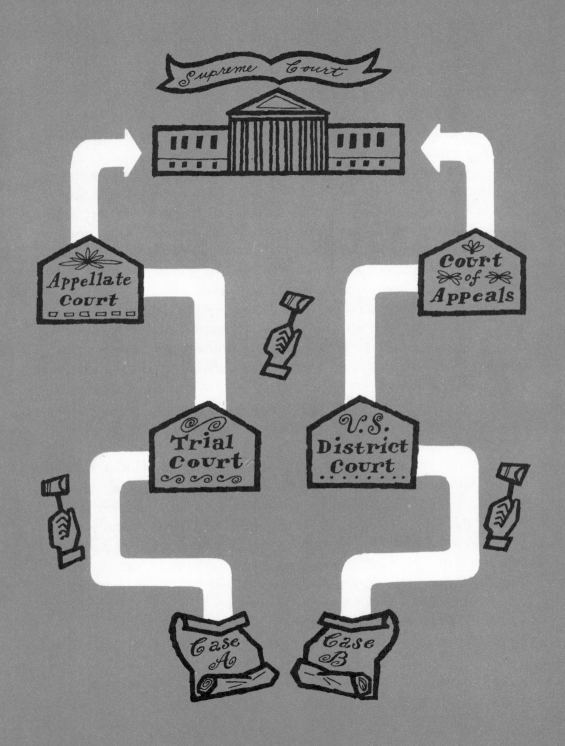

its territories, there is a federal **Court of Appeals** to hear cases from District Courts. Usually the Court of Appeals has the final word in a federal case.

As the Supreme Court can hear only a limited number of cases, it must by necessity decide lawsuits that raise problems of great national importance.

Each year a hundred cases, or thereabouts, reach the Supreme Court **on appeal** from state and federal courts. The party who appeals is the **appellant;** the other party is the **appellee.** An appeal may be taken to the Supreme Court when the court below finds a federal law unconstitutional, or a state law contrary to the "supreme law of the land," and when certain cases involve railroad regulation, the antitrust laws, and the prosecution of federal crime. Some appeals go from a District Court right to the Supreme Court, leapfrogging over the Court of Appeals. If an appeal does not seem sufficiently important, the Supreme Court dismisses it "for want of a substantial federal question."

Something over a hundred cases come to the high court on **writ of certiorari** (pronounced *sir-she-oh-*RAY-*ree*). If the loser in the court below thinks the judge has wrongly applied a federal law or overlooked a right guaranteed by the Constitution, he may petition the Court to issue a writ of this kind, ordering the lower court to send up the record of the case to the Supreme Court for review. The parties in such a case are the **petitioner** and the **respondent.**

Hundreds of petitions pile in to the Supreme Court, and all are carefully considered. Many must be denied. This does not necessarily mean that the petitions lack merit. Rather, other cases may raise issues of greater public importance, or perhaps the Court is waiting for the question to be presented more clearly in some later case. But if at least four of the nine Justices vote to do so, the Supreme Court

9

hears the case. Usually the case involves an important matter such as a conflict in the rulings of two federal courts, doubt as to the fairness of some trial procedure, or a disputed point that is holding up enforcement of an important law.

A few cases come to the Supreme Court by other paths. A Court of Appeals may **certify** a case to the Supreme Court, asking how to proceed. A person confined in violation of federal law may ask to be released on a **writ of habeas corpus.** And when one state sues another — over a boundary line or water rights, for example — it does so in the Supreme Court, without going through the lower courts.

Taking a case to the highest court of the land costs money. Various legal papers must be prepared, and forty printed copies must be supplied for the Justices, the Court's files, and other uses. Printing and filing fees may run to a thousand dollars, not counting the services of a lawyer.

How about a fellow who doesn't have a thousand dollars? He can apply to the Court **in forma pauperis** — as a poor man. Every year several hundred people do. Many are prisoners. They pound out their pleas on a battered typewriter, or a "jailhouse lawyer" does it for them. There's such a man in almost every prison, studying law to pass the time until his sentence has been served. Though most prisoners' petitions are turned down, a few are granted. The Supreme Court then pays for printing the legal papers, and appoints a lawyer to represent the prisoner. Grave wrongs have been corrected in this way.

Even an Act of Congress or an order by the President may be set aside by the Supreme Court if it is found to be in disagreement with the "higher law" of the Constitution. But the Court does not throw out as many laws of Congress as it once did. It is inclined to harmonize them, whenever possible, with the Constitution.

The Court's work consists mostly in deciding where justice lies in important controversies that involve the meaning of the laws.

Some things the Court won't do. It won't give even the government an **advisory opinion,** saying what the law would be if this or that came to pass. It won't hear a **friendly suit** merely for the purpose of testing a law. The opposing parties in a case must be battling for real stakes. Better decisions seem to result when they are made for the purpose of settling the controversies of real life.

Other names for the Supreme Court are the High Tribunal, the Supreme Bench, and the Court of Last Resort. The Court might well be called the Great Umpire. It doesn't pitch or go to bat, but it calls the plays.

11

Who Serves with the Court?

When a Supreme Court Justice retires, resigns, or dies, the President then in office names a new one. The name goes to the United States Senate, which ordinarily confirms, or approves, the proposed Justice. If the Senate should not approve, the President sends another name to it.

Some Justices go to the Court from a private law office or the bench of a lower court. Others have been governors and congressmen or members of the President's Cabinet — perhaps Attorney General. One Chief Justice, William Howard Taft, was a former President. By custom, the Court includes some men with executive and legislative experience and others with judicial experience. The Supreme Court is not merely a law court for settling private disputes; it is a judgment place for deciding the law in questions of wide public interest.

12

The Court speaks for a nation of continental size. There are likely to be one or two Justices from each region: New England, the Middle Atlantic States, the South, the Midwest, and the West. A typical Justice is in his fifties when appointed. The average age of the Court as a whole is around sixty-two.

A newly appointed Justice, like all government officials, swears to support and defend the Constitution. He also takes a judicial oath, promising to carry out his duties impartially, to "administer justice without respect to persons," and to "do equal right to the poor and to the rich." When he puts on his black robe and becomes a Justice, he leaves active party politics behind.

A friend once asked a Supreme Court Justice, "Does a man become any different when he puts on a gown?"

"If he is any good, he does," replied the Justice.

13

The Independent Judiciary

A Justice can state his opinion honestly, without fear that he will be punished for it. His salary can't be cut. He holds office "during good behavior." Practically speaking, that means all his life or till he retires. No Supreme Court Justice has ever been removed for misconduct. A Justice doesn't have to worry about making a living when he leaves the job.

The provisions about a Justice's salary and term of office were put in the Constitution so that the judicial branch might be truly independent, not only of the executive and legislative branches, but of all the various interests that appear before the Court. Judges are umpires. They must be free to call the plays as they see them.

The Justice and His Job

A Justice is never at a loss for summer reading. Petitions follow him to the beach and the mountains. He has weighty volumes to wade through in preparation for cases that are coming up.

Utilities

Flood Control

Banking

Taxes

Crop Quotas

Labor

strike

Each fall the Justices visit the White House and tell the President the Court is sitting. The Supreme Court term runs from the first Monday in October till June or later. Fifteen hundred appeals and petitions, more or less, will be considered. Some 250 cases will be decided. The records of a single case run anywhere from a few booklets to a five-foot shelf. Each Justice must make up his mind on every case. He reads at home morning and night, on taxes, money and banking, utility regulation, antitrust prosecutions, crop quotas, labor relations, flood control, civil liberties — whatever is before the Court to be decided.

The salary of an Associate Justice is $35,000 a year. Taxes may cut about $10,000 from his take-home pay. He can retire on full pay at

15

sixty-five, after serving fifteen years as a federal judge, or at seventy after ten years' service.

The Chief Justice receives $35,500 and has such extra duties as administering much detail work for the Court and presiding over the Judicial Council of the United States, which deals with administrative problems in all the court circuits.

Each Justice furnishes his own uniform, the "uniform of justice." His judicial robe of fine silk faille costs about $130. Perhaps, when he was appointed, his friends gave him one as a going-away present. He puts it on in the robing room before entering the courtroom. Under it he wears an ordinary suit, sometimes with a lightweight jacket.

Working conditions are pleasant. In the Supreme Court Building a Justice has a three-room suite: an oak-paneled office with fireplace and shower, his secretary's office, and a room for his two law clerks, who are probably honor graduates from his favorite law school. They are with him for a year, gaining experience and finding what he wants among the two hundred thousand books in the law library upstairs.

The dining room is upstairs, too. During the half hour for lunch a Justice has a snack, such as crackers and milk or a sandwich, with his **brethren.** To most people they are Mr. Justice Burton or Mr. Justice Whittaker, but he calls them My Brother Burton or My Brother Whittaker. Sometimes he may lunch in his chambers with a guest.

On the job he sees many people other than Justices. There are the clerk and his assistants, who receive legal documents and keep the calendar. The reporter of decisions sees the *United States Reports* (the Court's opinions) into print. The press officer supplies information to the Washington correspondents of the various newspapers. The marshal is in charge of the building. Working with the marshal are police officers, pages, switchboard operators, janitors, and a man to repair chipped and broken marble.

A Justice used to spend part of the year traveling a circuit and hearing cases. He no longer does this, but he still has special responsibilities for one or two of the eleven judicial circuits. Lawyers from his circuit call at his suite, and even at his summer home, asking him to take action in some emergency. Perhaps a lawyer has a client in a cell on death row, and nothing can save him unless the Justice **stays,** or holds up, the execution while a petition to the Supreme Court is prepared. If the request seems reasonable, the Justice may grant it, generally until the Court has acted on the prisoner's petition.

Justices are people, and however dignified a Justice looks on the bench, he has a sense of humor. Once a lawyer was arguing his case so forcefully that his false teeth flew out in the middle of a sentence. He caught them in midair, put them back, and went on. None of the Justices gave the slightest sign of noticing, until they were back in the robing room. Then they all broke out laughing together.

They tell jokes on themselves, too. One joke is about a lawyer who was spelling out the ABC's of his case.

"You might take it for granted this Court knows some simple law," suggested a Justice.

"Your Honor," said the lawyer, "that was the mistake I made in the court below."

Opinion Monday

Opinion Monday is the most interesting time to see the Court. This occasion is also called decision day or judgment day.

The Supreme Court **sits** two weeks, hearing cases and conferring, then usually **recesses** two weeks while the Justices write **opinions.** An opinion sums up the facts of a case and gives reasons for the Court's decision. Each Monday noon while the Court is sitting, the latest opinions are announced, or **handed down.** They make newspaper headlines Monday afternoon and Tuesday morning.

Millions of older Americans remember May 24, 1937, when Justice Benjamin N. Cardozo gave the Court's opinion upholding the Social Security Act. The Constitution says that Congress may tax and spend for the "general welfare of the United States." Does this include taxing payrolls and pay checks to provide benefits to people after they retire? The Court said it does.

More Americans than ever were then living in cities. Older people found it harder to make a living. Their number was increasing. The hope behind social security, said Mr. Justice Cardozo, was to "save men and women from the rigors of the poorhouse as well as from the haunting fear that such a lot awaits them when journey's end is near."

Another memorable Monday fell on May 17, 1954, when Chief Justice Earl Warren read the Court's unanimous decision in *Brown* v. *Board of Education of Topeka*. Linda Brown was an eleven-year-old Negro schoolgirl. By long custom she had been assigned to a separate school with others of her race. Suits had been brought in behalf of Linda and other pupils in various states, asking that they be admitted to unsegregated schools.

The tall, white-haired Chief Justice spoke quietly for half an hour. Calling education "the very foundation of good citizenship," he said it is "a right which must be made available to all on equal terms." He read the Court's conclusions, that "separate educational facilities are inherently unequal," and that children like Linda were "deprived of the equal protection of the laws guaranteed by the Fourteenth Amendment" to the Constitution.

An hour later the Voice of America was broadcasting the Court's decision to the world in thirty-four languages. The momentous task of desegregation had begun.

A Day in the Supreme Court

Every year hundreds of thousands of visitors see the Supreme Court. They can't all be there on opinion Monday, but there's something worth seeing almost any time.

Cross the grassy plaza east of the Capitol, and you come to a dazzling white marble building. Among the tourists, especially in the spring, are groups of young people in sports attire, accompanied by their teachers. You see them climbing the steps to the columned entrance-way, and over it you read the words: EQUAL JUSTICE UNDER LAW.

This is the spacious home the Supreme Court has occupied since

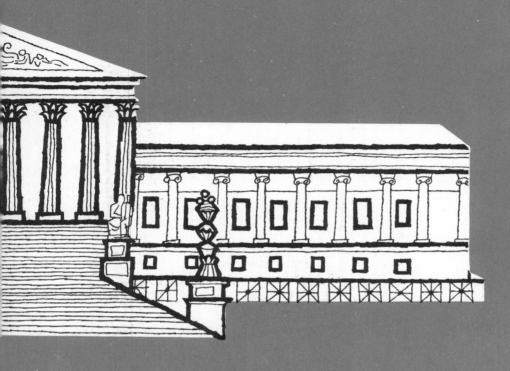

it moved from cramped quarters in the Capitol in 1935. The building has five stories at the center, and lower wings on each side.

Down the main corridor, past double rows of marble columns, is the courtroom. There may be a short wait to see it. The line forming on the right is for those who walk through for a look. If you want to sit and listen, line up on the left. Better be there before eleven, if it's opinion Monday. People start moving in about that time, two by two. Before court opens at noon, there is time to admire what has been called America's most impressive public room.

Mahogany furnishings, deep red curtains, and the brown and yellow tints of a marble colonnade blend pleasingly. High windows draw your eyes to the richly adorned ceiling and the carved frieze

with its procession of great lawgivers, including Moses, Confucius, Justinian, Blackstone, and America's own John Marshall.

There are benches and chairs for three hundred or more persons. The railed-off area up front is for the **bar** and the **press**: the lawyers and newspapermen. The lawyers' desks are supplied with quills made of white goose feathers; they are more for old times' sake than for writing. Beyond is the clerk's desk at one side, the marshal's desk at the other. In the center, the Justices' bench rises four feet from the floor against a backdrop of velvet curtains.

Nine upholstered swivel chairs of uneven height are waiting there.

When the building was opened, the Justices were presented with tall wooden chairs, handsomely carved and exactly alike, but so uncomfortable that the Court members went on sitting in the chairs they liked best. Now, each Justice chooses from the several types of chair available when he takes his seat on the Court.

At ten minutes to twelve, by the clock over the Chief Justice's chair, lawyers are rummaging through briefcases and conferring together. Pages in serge suits and knickers are putting paper and pencils at each Justice's place.

At twelve sharp, a gavel falls. While everyone stands, the velvet

23

curtains part and the robed Justices come out to their places.

The Court crier says, "The Honorable, the Chief Justice and the Associate Justices of the Supreme Court of the United States." He pauses, and cries, "Oyez, Oyez, Oyez!" (Oyez means "Hear ye!") "All persons having business before the Honorable, the Supreme Court of the United States are admonished to draw near and give their attention, for the Court is now sitting. God save the United States and this Honorable Court."

Another gavel blow, and you sit down and try to put names and faces together. At the center of the bench is the Chief Justice. The other Justices sit near him in order of **seniority,** or length of service — those next to him are his two most experienced colleagues. Here's the line-up from your left to right: 7, 5, 3, 1, Chief Justice, 2, 4, 6, 8.

If it's decision day, the Chief Justice nods to whoever has written the **opinion of the Court** in the first case. This opinion has been accepted by a majority of the Justices. Perhaps it is followed by a **concurring opinion,** in which another Justice has come to the same conclusions by different reasoning; and a **dissenting opinion** by anyone who believes the case should have been decided the other way.

Prior to the announcing of opinions, attorneys are admitted to the **bar of the Court.** A lawyer is eligible for admission if he has had the same privilege in the highest court of his state for three years. He is introduced by another lawyer, welcomed by the Chief Justice, and sworn in at the clerk's desk. Now he can argue cases before the Supreme Court — and hang a certificate in his office to prove it.

The rest of the afternoon is devoted to hearing cases to be decided. There is no jury, and no dock where the prisoner stands forlornly. This is a lawyers' court. Cases come here from the lower courts for final decision. Each side usually has an hour for argument. The written arguments are already in. This is the lawyers' one chance to speak their pieces.

Daniel Webster used to appear before the Court in a long blue coat with brass buttons. Chief Justice Taft sent a lawyer home to put on a vest. Most suits don't have vests nowadays, but anyone addressing the Supreme Court feels better in a dark suit with the jacket buttoned. Government attorneys and some others argue cases in cutaway coats and morning trousers. The Court is always willing to hear a woman lawyer, but she must remove her hat.

An attorney addresses the Court as "Your Honors." Notice how fast he thinks on his feet. The Justices fire questions whenever they please. The lawyer replies without losing the thread of his argument, or maybe he drops the old thread and picks up a new one. A question may be a clue to the way the Court is thinking. A light flashes on the rostrum in front of the lawyer's notes when his time is running out; when the second light flashes, his time has expired and he sits down at a nod from the Chief Justice.

There is a half hour for lunch at two o'clock — time for you to have a bite in the cafeteria downstairs, and a look at the bronze and marble stairway at either end of the building. Up and up it spirals, with seemingly nothing to support it.

After lunch, the Court picks up where it left off. One case follows another without delay. Pages carry messages from one Justice to another, and run to the library for law books. Sightseers come and go — ordinary Americans.

Many a case argued in this magnificent chamber has to do with people

like Thomas Lee Causby, a North Carolina chicken farmer. His hens began flying into walls after the farm next door was turned into a military airport, and bombers, fighters, and transports with glaring lights went zooming over all night long. He lost ten chickens in one night. In *United States* v. *Causby* the Supreme Court decided that the government, in making the chicken farm useless, had taken private property for public use and must pay the owner fairly.

At 4:30 sharp, the Court adjourns — and no tarrying. Grover Cleveland, a former President, once was arguing a case at the end of the day. He told Chief Justice Melville W. Fuller, whom he had appointed when he was President, that he would be through in two minutes. "Mr. Cleveland," said the Chief Justice courteously, "we will hear you tomorrow morning."

A Continuing

Constitutional Convention

The United States Constitution runs to about seven thousand words. A radio broadcaster could read it aloud in forty minutes.

The President, it says, "shall hold his office during the term of four years." Neither a state nor the United States shall "grant any title of nobility." Easy, isn't it? Let's go on.

No person shall "be deprived of life, liberty, or property, without due process of law." Hey, wait! Let's look up **due process of law.** The dictionary says it's "that course of legal proceedings that is in accordance with the law of the land." And the "law of the land" goes back to Magna Charta in the year 1215. Maybe we need more than a dictionary to understand the Constitution.

For $6.25 the Government Printing Office in Washington will send a person *The Constitution of the United States of America: Analysis and Interpretation,* prepared by the Library of Congress. It has 1,361 pages, and lawyers love it. An explanation of "due process" takes 189 of its pages.

The book sums up briefly what the Supreme Court has said about the Constitution. Its fine print tells the reader where to look for the Court's full opinions. The case of the cedar and apple trees is *Miller* v. *Schoene,* 276 U.S. 272. This means it is in Volume 276 of the *United States Reports,* beginning on page 272. The law library in your local county courthouse may have it.

John Marshall, famous former Chief Justice, once wrote, "We must never forget that it is *a constitution* we are expounding." The Constitu-

27

tion, he said, provides the "great outlines" of our government, but the details remain to be filled in.

The Supreme Court has been called a continuing Constitutional Convention, marking out the boundaries between the power of the states and the nation, the President and Congress, and the individual citizen and the government. As cases are decided, some fall this way, some that way. Gradually a line of separation in powers appears. It is a fairer boundary than could have been drawn without the help of actual cases.

The Supreme Court's opinions fill more than 350 volumes. Don't try to read them all. Here are a few guideposts to help you get your bearings.

One thing to keep in mind is that the Supreme Court helps maintain the system of balances on which the government rests.

Checks and balances are built into the Constitution. Its framers believed that if all power lay with Congress, or the President, or the courts, there would soon be a government not of laws but of men. They provided for a **separation of powers** so that, if one branch of government went too far, another would check or balance it.

President and Congress

A congressman must represent his district first of all, and a senator his state; but the President, like the Supreme Court, is free to speak for the nation. Congress can pass no law over his veto, except by a two-thirds vote.

The President may call out troops, says the Supreme Court, to keep the lanes of commerce open. As Commander in Chief, he has vast wartime powers. But it's to Congress he must look for money and for the laws he wants passed. This division of authority helps keep the balance.

The Supreme Court tips the scales now this way, now that. It tends to support the President in dealings with foreign countries, but to back up Congress at home. During the Korean War, when a steel strike seemed near, President Truman put Army men in charge to keep the mills running. The Court said he had no emergency power to do this on his own; it was a job for the nation's lawmakers.

29

State versus State

Chicago once made a river run backwards. Marvels of engineering turned the Chicago River away from Lake Michigan. Boats sailed across Illinois and down the Mississippi to New Orleans. The city tapped Lake Michigan for water, and flushed its sewage into the Mississippi River.

Then came the complications. Down went the lake's water level. Docks and warehouses farther north were left high and dry. Fishing grounds disappeared. Shoreline homes stared at mud flats. Wisconsin sued Illinois for letting Chicago take the water. Several other states joined in.

The case of *Wisconsin* v. *Illinois* went direct to the Supreme Court. Many months were needed for hearing evidence — more time than could be spared by the Court. In such cases the Court appoints an outstanding attorney as a **special master** to find the facts and make recommendations. This time it chose Charles Evans Hughes, a former Justice who later became Chief Justice. After the Hughes report was in, the opposing lawyers told the Court why they were for or against his ideas.

The Court handed down its decree in 1930. Chicago was entitled to enough water for navigation, but no more. However, the people's health was safeguarded. The city was given eight years in which to build sewage treatment plants. Meanwhile its water ration was gradually to be cut.

This dispute between states was settled peaceably by the Supreme Court. Nations have gone to war for less, and come out worse than did Wisconsin and Illinois.

The Federal Union

America's thirteen original states felt a strong need to be able to trade freely with one another, without barriers of any kind. A meeting on this subject by representatives of Maryland and Virginia led to the Constitutional Convention in Philadelphia in 1787. From this came the Constitution of the United States.

John Marshall, the great Chief Justice of early days, gave the Constitution a **broad construction** — a very general meaning — not a **strict construction** — a limited meaning.

The Constitution gives Congress power to make whatever laws are "necessary and proper" to enable the federal government to use its other powers. This is the **elastic clause.** It stretches what Congress can do.

John Marshall put it this way: "Let the end be legitimate, let it be within the scope of the Constitution, and all means which are appropriate, which are plainly adapted to that end, which are not prohibited, but consist with the letter and spirit of the Constitution, are constitutional."

In other words, Congress was free to pass any reasonable laws to carry out the purposes for which the Union was formed, provided it acted in harmony with the intent of the Constitution.

Marshall also wrote the opinion in *Gibbons* v. *Ogden*, the Steamboat Case. Gibbons wanted to carry passengers from New Jersey to New York in his new-fangled boat, but Ogden's group alone had the right to operate from New York State. Gibbons won the case. Closing New York Harbor to competing steamboats and allowing Ogden alone to carry passengers would interfere with commerce between the states, said Marshall.

31

When Congress makes rules for commerce between the states, it uses the **commerce power.** Supreme Court rulings down the years have brought many things within this power: not only buying, selling, and navigation, but the tariff, railroads, electricity, pipelines, the telephone and telegraph, manufacturing, mining, agriculture, radio, television, and airborne commerce.

A laundry in Memphis, Tennessee, sent ten drivers into Mississippi to pick up and deliver bundles. Mississippi slapped a $50 tax on each truck, though laundries located in the state paid only $8. The Supreme Court has thrown out many laws like this. If allowed to stand, such laws would lead to tax wars. Soon every state would put up tariff walls against its neighbors.

The states do need money for roads, schools, and all the expenses of local government. And the Supreme Court upholds their right to lay taxes that are fair to all and not too much of a burden on the nation's commerce. Tax cases are complicated. How would you tax railroad cars that are here today and gone tomorrow — or a passenger plane that streaks across the state in thirty minutes? States have tried various ways. In case of dispute, the Supreme Court decides whether the tax is fair to all concerned — to the state, to the company, and to other states in which the company does business.

You have seen motor trucks with registration plates from several states. A fee is paid for each plate — a sort of state tax for wear and tear on the highways. Some states limit the size and weight of trucks,

or make them use certain roads. The Court has held that a state can make rules like these under the **police power.** This phrase means something quite different from the power of the state police. It means a state's broad power to protect the people's health, safety, and welfare. But the police power has limits. Illinois told one trucking line to keep out of the state entirely, and the Supreme Court said that interfered with Uncle Sam's interstate commerce rules.

When a state's police power and the nation's commerce power meet head on, the Supreme Court asks: Which has the greater interest here, the state or the nation? Did Congress intend to regulate this kind of commerce or to let the states do it? Does the state law help or hinder the federal law? Perhaps there is room for both.

Because of the federal commerce power, we can cross the continent without passports and do business everywhere in the forty-eight states. We have supermarkets, network shows, mass production, and high living standards. Yet we are not under the rule of one all-powerful government, for most everyday affairs come within the police power of state and local governments. The federal Union rests on balanced powers like these. And the Supreme Court is the balance wheel.

Property Rights vs. Social Welfare

Words change their meanings with time and circumstance. Take the Constitution's Fifth Amendment clause, "nor shall any person . . . be deprived of life, liberty, or property, without due process of law." Americans of the year 1800 used to say, "it means they can't hang, jail, or fine you without a fair trial." Later on, many Northerners came to believe it meant that no one could rightly be robbed of his liberty and made a slave. But the South took its stand with Chief Justice Roger B. Taney, who ruled that the Negro slave Dred Scott was still a slave after living on free soil. A slave was property, said Taney, and to take away his owner's property because he took it where he pleased "could hardly be dignified with the name of due process of law."

Due process was already guaranteed by the federal government, but after the Civil War the Fourteenth Amendment made it binding on the states. Still its meaning depended on time and circumstance. Most Justices of 1905 had grown up on farms. They were used to long hours, and had little patience with a New York law calling for a ten-hour working day in bakeries. They claimed that such a law took away a baker's liberty without due process of law — his liberty to work as long as he chose.

Some years later Congress passed a law forbidding goods made by children under fourteen to be traded between the states. The Court struck down this law. It said the law interfered with matters properly left to the states.

Today these last two cases are remembered for the dissenting opinions of Justice Oliver Wendell Holmes. He pointed out that liberty to do as one likes is interfered with by school laws and many other laws, and that a reasonable man might consider the bakery law proper on the score of health. As for the child labor law, Holmes claimed it did not meddle with anything belonging to the states. They might do as they liked at home, he said, but when they sent the product of ruined lives across the state line, they were no longer within their rights.

One day in 1908 a most unusual brief was filed with the Court in support of Oregon's ten-hour working day for women. A page or two of law was followed by a hundred pages of medical opinions regarding the harm done women by long hours of factory work. It won the case, and a brief like this is still called a **Brandeis brief** for Louis D. Brandeis, who prepared it. He was later a Justice, and usually saw eye to eye with Holmes. They were forerunners of what has been called the Constitutional Revolution of 1937.

The case of Elsie Parrish, a hotel chambermaid, led the way. She sued for $14.50 a week under the Washington state minimum-wage

10-HOUR DAY·

MINIMUM WAGE·

law. Her employer replied that the law took away his liberty to make a contract, without due process of law, and he quoted the Supreme Court to prove it. But America was digging out of a depression, and the Court had changed. Chief Justice Hughes said reasonable regulation of wages *was* due process of law. He thought the liberty that mattered most to Elsie Parrish was the kind that protected her health and welfare.

So, besides getting Elsie Parrish her $14.50, her case did a service to forty-eight states. It enlarged their police power. Other Court decisions soon followed, letting the federal government tackle great national problems under the commerce power. Among them were flood control, the marketing of crops, and collective bargaining between employers and wage-earners.

Thus the Court came to serve as a balance wheel between individual property rights and the welfare of society as a whole.

State-Federal Cooperation

State and federal powers under the Constitution are not necessarily against each other. More and more, the states and the nation pull together for the common good. They share the cost of highways and hospitals. The federal wage-hour law is mostly enforced in state courts. Congress has a right to regulate insurance, but actually leaves it to the states.

Federal laws back up state laws in the fight against crime. It is a federal offense to cross a state line with a stolen car, a sawed-off shotgun, or a kidnapped person. Congress has made these things forbidden articles of commerce. The Supreme Court has upheld the laws.

Recently the Court has staked out broader police powers than ever for the states. Provided they don't play favorites among producers, states may halt wasteful tapping of such resources as natural gas. They may clear away slums and make their cities "beautiful as well as healthy, spacious as well as clean, well-balanced as well as carefully patrolled."

The Fourth Branch of Government

To the three branches of government — legislative, executive, judicial — some people add a fourth: the **administrative agencies.**

Some of these agencies have developed within the executive branch of the government — such as the Civil Aeronautics Board in the Department of Commerce and the Immigration and Naturalization Service in the Department of Justice. Other agencies are independent regulatory commissions. These began with the federal Interstate Commerce Commission, which approves railroad and telephone rates. The federal Securities and Exchange Commission keeps an eye on the stock markets. The Federal Communications Commission licenses radio and TV stations.

There have been other agencies to mobilize men and materials for war and defense. These agencies stem from the vast **war power** — a combination of various powers of the President and Congress.

Administrative agencies fill a modern need for expert handling of complicated problems. But they don't always agree with our old idea of government in three packages. An agency may have power to make rules that have the force of law. Does that make it legislative? If an agency makes rules, it must see that they are obeyed. Does that make it executive? Perhaps it holds hearings, and hands down decisions. Does that make it judicial? Actually, an administrative agency may be a little of all three.

Where, then, are the time-honored checks and balances? How are administrative agencies kept from abusing their power? The Supreme Court searches for answers. It is helping build a new set of balances.

As the Court sees it, the lawmaking power belongs to Congress. Even Congress can't give away its power without marking out the limits. A law setting up an agency should answer these questions: What is the job to be done? Who shall do it? When may he act? How far may he go?

An agency operates under certain rules. When it holds a hearing, the persons who are concerned are entitled to due notice and a chance to be heard. The **trial examiner,** or **hearing officer,** who sits as a judge, is independent of those who investigate and prosecute. They cannot fire him for deciding against them.

Appeals from orders of administrative agencies are taken to court on various grounds. When a case reaches the Supreme Court, the Court asks: Has the agency violated its own rules of procedure? Has it gone beyond the authority marked out by Congress? Has it denied anyone a constitutional right? If not, the agency is usually upheld. Its expert findings command respect and are not set aside unless they are so contrary to the evidence as to be "unfair and unreasonable."

Liberty versus Authority

The big car screeched to a halt at the McNabb settlement in the Tennessee mountains.

Four men jumped out. "All right, boys, federal officers!"

Branches crashed underfoot, shadowy figures melted away, and all was still.

The revenuers began tipping over cans of moonshine whiskey. *Plop!* A boulder landed at Officer Leeper's feet. He went after the culprit, flashlight in hand. As he searched the family burying ground, a shot came from the darkness, and he fell, mortally wounded.

Who of that numerous mountain clan had pulled the trigger? It was hard to say. The officers dragged two brothers and a cousin from hiding and took them to Chattanooga, twelve miles away. The McNabb boys had never before been that far from home. They had quit school in the third grade, and they had no lawyer to advise them. After being questioned all night and all day, they signed "confessions" and were speedily convicted.

Now, it's important to punish the guilty — but also to spare the innocent. What chance had three McNabbs against the power of the United States? You will find the answer in *McNabb* v. *United States*, 318 U. S. 332, where the Supreme Court decided against the convictions, and spoke out for "civilized standards of procedure."

We are reminded in the Court's opinion that an accused person must be taken promptly before a judge, who may let him out on bail or dismiss the charges. This procedure guards against the "third degree" and forced confessions. It discourages "easy but self-defeating ways in which brutality is substituted for brains as an instrument of crime detection."

41

The Court attaches much importance to proper procedure. "The history of liberty has largely been the history of observance of procedural safeguards," says the McNabb opinion. Five of the Constitution's first ten amendments — our **Bill of Rights** — deal with procedures. Among them are the right to have a lawyer, to face one's accusers in open court, and to be tried by an impartial jury.

Under the Fifth Amendment no one is compelled to be a witness against himself. This is the **privilege against self-incrimination.** It was won, says Justice William O. Douglas, in the long struggle to be safe from torture. People often assume that anyone who "takes the Fifth" must be guilty. But that is not the Supreme Court's view. As Justice Tom C. Clark put it recently, "A witness may have a reasonable fear of prosecution and yet be innocent of any wrongdoing." The privilege, he said, serves to protect the innocent who might otherwise come under suspicion because of unusual circumstances.

The Constitution's Bill of Rights lists things the federal government can't do. Is the Bill also binding on the states? Yes, in part, says the Court. Some Justices consider the "due process" clause of the Four-

freedom of religion

free press

teenth Amendment a guarantee of the whole Bill of Rights, but the Court's majority has held that a state may follow other procedures if they provide the fundamentals of a fair trial. A state, if it chooses, may try certain cases with a jury of less than twelve. It may try some lesser offenses even without a jury. But if it keeps all members of one race off juries, that is no longer due process of law.

If a man is on trial and too poor to hire a lawyer, then the state must find him one, at least if he is accused of a crime punishable by death. If he makes an unwilling confession, and it is used against him, his conviction may not stick.

The **First Amendment freedoms** — those guaranteed in the First Amendment to the Constitution — are freedom of religion, free speech, a free press, and the right of assembly and petition. The Supreme Court has decided that neither the federal government nor the states may interfere with these fundamental rights.

Newton Cantwell and his sons Jesse and Russell belonged to a group called Jehovah's Witnesses. While offering religious books for sale in New Haven, Connecticut, they were arrested. The charge was soliciting without a certificate from the state public welfare council.

free speech · assembly & petition

Now, this body had power to approve religious causes it liked and to turn down others. The Supreme Court ruled that a state can't pick and choose among religions. It must treat them all alike. *Cantwell* v. *Connecticut* has become a foundation stone of religious liberty in every state.

Justice Holmes used to say that to many people free speech means, "You may say anything that I don't think shocking." But the real test of free speech, he added, is "freedom for the thought we hate."

Free speech and the other freedoms sometimes have hard sledding in stormy times. The Supreme Court has been called the "conscience of the American people." It is the wee voice whispering to the "better angels of our nature" to restore the delicate balance between liberty and authority.

After the Civil War the legislature of strife-torn Missouri would not let a man follow certain callings until he swore he had never helped the Confederacy. Father Cummings refused to take the oath. The Supreme Court upheld him. The legislature, it said, was punishing him without a judicial trial, by denying him the right to be a priest.

Ninety years later, in 1957, the Court made headlines by saying Congress is not a law enforcement or trial agency for punishing people. John T. Watkins, a labor organizer, had run afoul of a congressional investigating committee. He had answered questions about himself, but he had refused to name friends who once were Communists. So he was in contempt of Congress and liable to a year in jail.

The Supreme Court said Congress' power to investigate is broad, but not unlimited. It may ask all questions necessary for making laws and improving the efficiency of government. But "there is no congressional power to expose for the sake of exposure." That would tread on the First Amendment freedoms. And so Watkins went free.

How Cases Are Decided

The hardest part of the Supreme Court Justices' job is the Friday conference. At 11 a. m. the Justices take their places at the table under the crystal chandelier in the book-lined conference room. No one else may enter. Everything said there is a secret, but from what Justices have written we know in a general way how a conference goes.

The Chief Justice is at one end of the table; the others are grouped according to seniority. There is no page inside, so the "freshman" Justice acts as doorkeeper for messages. The order of business has sixty or seventy items, including appeals, petitions, and the cases argued during the week. The conference continues, with a break for lunch, often till half-past five or later.

A case is up for decision. The Chief Justice sums up the points at issue and his conclusions. Next the senior Associate Justice gives his views, and so on around the table. The freshman speaks last, but votes first so that he won't be unduly swayed by his seniors. Time is pressing. Some Chief Justices have allowed freer discussion than others, before taking a vote. There have been times when such hot words were spoken that on Monday morning the Chief asked the Justices to shake hands all around.

People sometimes say, "Judges are supposed to know what the law is. Why can't they agree?" But if the law were that simple, you could do without judges, according to Justice Felix Frankfurter. You'd punch holes in cards, feed them into an electronic machine, and get a decision. A judge starts out by matching the case at hand with others that have been decided according to certain rules of law. It's when the colors don't match that a judge's work really begins, Justice Benjamin Cardozo once said. Many cases involve more than one principle of

45

law. One interest is balanced against another. And of course the Supreme Court gets the hardest cases of all.

A Justice votes on the decision of a case without knowing who is to write the Court's opinion. He may be it. After the conference the Chief Justice prepares assignment lists, and his brethren have their work cut out for the recess between sittings. When the Chief Justice is in the minority, the senior Justice on the majority side asks someone to write the opinion.

A full-dress opinion may call for days of laborious research and brain-cudgeling. The Justice outlines his ideas. Then, surrounded by heaps of books with markers showing, he writes or dictates a first draft. It goes to a print shop right in the building, to make sure nothing leaks out ahead of time.

Each Justice receives proof sheets of the printed opinion. If he likes his brother's work, he returns it to him with a comment like "Yes, indeed!" or "Good sense and good law." If he would like some changes, he writes a memorandum or drops into his brother's office for a chat. The writer of the opinion makes the changes if he can, but it's not always possible to get a majority of the Justices to agree on the same wording. Some of them may approve of the result, but may write opinions of their own — concurring opinions.

A dissenting opinion — one that takes the opposite view — often carries more punch than a majority opinion. The writer doesn't have to please anyone but himself, though one or more of his brethren may join with him or write dissents of their own. Dissenting opinions safeguard our constitutional system by putting majority decisions to the test of criticism. They are part of the record, and may even gain the approval of some future Court.

After a majority opinion has made the rounds and been revised, it comes up for a vote at a Friday conference. If the final form is acceptable, it is then announced on some early opinion Monday. The Court's opinion is directly binding on the parties in dispute. Its main thread of reasoning is woven into the rules of the law. Lawyers will mention it in their briefs, and judges in their decisions.

Can the Supreme Court make its decisions stick? That was settled back in 1824, when an Ohio state official lost a tax case in the Supreme Court, but refused to return $120,000 to the winner. The federal courts went into action. A United States marshal jailed the official for contempt of court, took a key from his pocket, and removed the money from the treasury, all by due process of law.

In 1957, President Eisenhower told the nation, "The very basis of our individual rights and freedoms rests upon the certainty that the President and the executive branch of government will support and ensure the carrying out of the decisions of the federal courts."

The Court's Secret Weapon

Umpires are not always popular, and neither is the Supreme Court. In every case it decides, there is a loser.

"Our people often criticize the Court and disagree with it, but they have a respect and reverence for it, born of decades of experience," Justice Douglas told an audience in India.

The Court has weathered every storm, including controversies with Presidents as popular as Jefferson, Jackson, Lincoln, and the two Roosevelts. Its prestige has grown through the years.

The Court has been placed beyond the reach of day-by-day politics, as Justice Robert H. Jackson once pointed out, so that it can

47

stand guard over fundamental rights without depending on the outcome of elections. It protects the rights of minorities. Everyone belongs to a minority at one time or another: if not a religious or racial minority, then a minority on some public question.

Justice Hugo L. Black has said, "No higher duty, no more solemn responsibility, rests upon this Court, than that of translating into living law and maintaining this constitutional shield deliberately planned and inscribed for the benefit of every human being subject to our Constitution — of whatever race, creed or persuasion."

A Supreme Court Justice goes to great lengths to avoid even the appearance of partiality. He **disqualifies** himself from sitting in a case if he has any possible interest in its outcome. Chief Justice Harlan F. Stone once owned shares of stock in a company that was charged with breaking the antitrust laws. He promptly sold his holdings and put the money into another company. Soon this company, too, was in trouble. The Chief Justice then sold his stock a second time, so that he could vote his beliefs with a clear conscience, if later he sat in judgment on the case.

48

When an umpire rules a home-town player out at third base, the crowd may yell that he needs glasses. Over the long pull, though, he commands respect if people know he is impartial.

So actually the Supreme Court's authority rests less on force than on its reputation for fairness. We look up to the Court as the highest source of the law of the land.

"No man or group is above the law," Justice Wiley B. Rutledge once said. "All are subject to its valid commands. So are the government and the courts."

JAL · JUSTICE · UNDER · LAW ·

Some Words the Court Uses

Act of Congress—a bill enacted into law by Congress

admiralty and maritime law—the law that federal courts apply in disputes arising out of navigation on the high seas and on inland waterways

advisory opinion—an opinion stating what the law would be in a situation that might possibly arise; never given by the Supreme Court

affirm—to declare a lower court's decision correct

antitrust laws—various acts of Congress which make it illegal for commercial companies to combine in a way that will hinder trade and commerce or stifle free competition

appeal—a proceeding to take a case to a higher court for review

appellant—one who appeals a case to a higher court

appellate court—one that reviews a lower court's proceedings and hears appeals from its decisions

appellee—one against whom an appeal is taken; the winner in the court below

bail—money or other security put up to free a person under arrest and guarantee his appearance for trial. The Eighth Amendment forbids excessive bail

Brandeis brief—a legal brief showing how a case affects health and welfare, or supplying other background facts; first used by Louis D. Brandeis, later a Supreme Court Justice

calendar—a list of cases set down for argument, in the order in which they are expected to be called

case—an action in court to protect rights or redress wrongs

certify—to send a Court of Appeals case to the Supreme Court, asking instructions

certiorari, writ of (*sir-she-oh-*RAY-*ree*)—an order to a lower court to send up the record of a case for review

civil case—one involving a dispute between persons, persons and governments, or governments; not a criminal case

civil law—a system of law growing out of Roman law, and followed in continental Europe and in Louisiana. "Civil" does not mean the same here as in "civil case" above

commerce power—Congress' constitutional power "to regulate commerce with foreign nations, and among the several states, and with the Indian tribes" (Article I, Section 8). By Supreme Court decisions, it includes commerce within a state which is commingled, or mixed, with interstate commerce

common law—a system of law common to all of England in the late Middle Ages, and since then shaped by court decisions in English-speaking countries and in our various states. In different senses, common law is contrasted with civil or Roman law; with statutory law as passed by legislative bodies; and with equity (see below)

concurring opinion—one agreeing with the result of another opinion in the same case, but stating the reasons separately

constitutional—agreeing with the Constitution; as, a law not in violation of its provisions. A constitutional government is one whose powers are limited by a constitution

constitutional law—principles that guide the Supreme Court in fixing the boundaries of the authority belonging to different branches of the government and to the states and the nation; and in balancing the interests of private property and social welfare and of the individual and the government

construction—finding out the meaning of a law or a constitutional provision. A criminal law is construed strictly, so that everyone may know exactly what is forbidden. The Constitution, being in general terms, receives a broader construction: a power not stated may be implied from one that is

contempt—disregard of a court's authority, or disobedience of its lawful orders. Refusal to answer the proper questions of a congressional committee is contempt of Congress

counsel—the lawyer or lawyers in a case; also the advice they give

court below—the lower court in which a case was last heard

court-martial—a trial in the armed forces under the Uniform Code of Military Justice. The Supreme Court has ruled that a person discharged from service is no longer subject to court-martial

Court of Appeals—a federal appellate court in one of the eleven circuits of the United States. It stands between the District Courts and the Supreme Court

criminal case—one in which the defendant is charged with breaking a law intended to protect the public from injury

decision—what a court decides in settling a case, as when the Supreme Court affirms or reverses the decision of a lower court or sends the case back for further proceedings. The Court's entire opinion is sometimes called a decision

decree—an order issued by a court of equity or admiralty after hearing a case. It sets forth the rights and duties of the parties

deny—to turn down a petition or other request

determination—a decision by a court or administrative agency

dismiss the charges—to drop a complaint against an arrested person for lack of evidence

disqualify—to make ineligible, as when a judge disqualifies himself from sitting in a case because of some possible interest in the outcome

dissenting opinion—one disagreeing with the opinion of the Court

District Court, United States—a court in which federal civil and criminal cases, as well as suits between citizens of different states, are tried. Each state has one or more District Courts

doctrine—a principle of law used in deciding cases

due process of law—reasonable procedures according to the law of the land, including a fair trial with opportunity to face one's accusers and be heard in defense. Interfering with freedom of speech, press, or religion is held to deprive people of liberty without due process of law

elastic clause—the one that stretches the power of Congress by giving it the right "to make all laws which shall be necessary and proper for carrying into execution the foregoing powers, and all other powers vested by this Constitution in the government of the United States, or in any department or officer thereof" (Article I, Section 8)

equity—a system of justice developed in English chancery courts to offer more flexible remedies than those available in common-law courts. An injunction ordering a person to stop doing something harmful, rather than waiting till the damage is done, is an example of equity. Another was the Supreme Court's decree limiting Chicago's use of water from Lake Michigan, but giving the city time to build sewage disposal plants. Our federal courts and many higher state courts hear cases in both law and equity

ex post facto law—a law making a crime of an action done in the past, or increasing the punishment for it. Neither the federal government nor the states may pass ex post facto laws (Article I, Sections 9 and 10)

federal question—one making it necessary to find out the meaning of a federal law, treaty, or constitutional provision in order to decide a case. Cases go from state courts to the Supreme Court only when a federal question arises

First Amendment freedoms—freedom of religion, free speech, a free press, and freedom to meet and petition the government for a redress of grievances. Free discussion is so vital in a democracy that the Supreme Court has held that neither the federal government nor a state may restrict it except when it creates "a clear and present danger" of bringing about serious evils which the government has a right to prevent

friendly suit—a suit to test a law. The parties are not real adversaries

general welfare clause—the opening clause of Article I, Section 8, empowering Congress "to lay and collect taxes, duties, imposts and excises, to pay the debts and provide for the common defense and general welfare of the United States." The Supreme Court has held that Congress may tax and spend for a purpose serving the general welfare, whether mentioned in the Constitution or not

government of limited powers—one limited by a written or unwritten constitution. Our federal government has limited powers over the states and the people

grand jury—see *jury*

habeas corpus—Latin for "you have the body." A writ of habeas corpus orders someone who is holding another person to bring him bodily into court. The judge then decides whether the prisoner is being lawfully detained and, if not, releases him

hearing officer—an officer, corresponding to a judge, who presides at administrative agency hearings; a trial examiner

holding—what the Court holds the law to be

indictment—an accusation by a grand jury, charging someone with a crime upon evidence presented by the public prosecutor

in forma pauperis—in the manner of a poor person. If permitted to sue this way, a person is not liable for costs

injunction—a court order forbidding someone to harm another person's interests

jeopardy—peril, such as the danger of punishment faced by a defendant on trial. No person may be twice put in jeopardy for the same federal offense (Fifth Amendment)

judgment—a court's decision or sentence of law

judicial power—power to decide cases and controversies under the laws

judicial review—the Court's examination of a law to find out whether it is in harmony with the Constitution or with federal laws and treaties. More broadly, judicial review means reconsidering a case decided in a lower court

jury—a body of impartial citizens who examine evidence placed before them, looking for the truth. A grand jury hears complaints and makes accusations of crime. A trial jury, or petit jury, determines the guilt or innocence of an

53

accused person

opinion Monday—a Monday when the Supreme Court is in session and hands down opinions

original jurisdiction—power to hear a case at the beginning. The Supreme Court has original jurisdiction when one of the parties is a state or a foreign diplomat (actually the State Department handles most disputes involving diplomats) In other cases, the Court has appellate jurisdiction; it hears cases on appeal

overrule—to reject the authority of an earlier decision by deciding the same question of law the opposite way

petitioner—one who asks the Court to use its authority, as by issuing a writ of certiorari, to bring a case from a lower court for review

police power—governmental power to protect the people's health, safety, and welfare. The Court has upheld various laws under a state's police power that might otherwise be an unwarranted interference with the federal commerce power or with individual property rights

political question—one to be settled by the legislative or executive branches of government, not by the Court. Examples: How long do the states have to ratify a proposed amendment to the Constitution? Is a treaty with another nation still in effect?

precedent—a court decision that serves as an example in deciding similar cases

procedural rights—in federal cases, the protection of procedures set forth in the Bill of Rights and in federal laws; in state cases, the fundamentals of a fair trial by due process of law

quorum—six of the nine Justices are a quorum for hearing and deciding cases. If the vote is a tie, the decision of the lower court stands, but the Supreme Court will consider rehearing the case. A state or federal law is never invalidated unless five or more Justices so vote

recess—an interval of two weeks or longer between sittings, when opinions are prepared

respondent—the party opposing the petitioner in a case

reverse—to set aside the judgment of a lower court

self-incrimination, privilege against—the right not to testify against oneself (Fifth Amendment)

separation of powers—division of governmental power among the legislative, executive, and judicial branches, so that one will check or balance another. James Madison, the "Father of the Constitution," said, "It may be a reflection on human nature that such devices should be necessary to control the abuses of government. But what is government itself but the greatest of all reflections on human nature? If men were angels, no government would be necessary."

session—each day's sitting of the Court

sitting—a session; an open meeting of the Court where business is conducted

Solicitor General—an officer of the Department of Justice, ranking next after the Attorney General. He represents the interests of the United States in cases before the Supreme Court

stay—to hold up or halt the carrying out of a judicial sentence

supreme law of the land—the Constitution, laws made in pursuance thereof, and treaties made under the authority of the United States; based on the supremacy clause in Article VI of the Constitution

term—the time when the Court is sitting or in recess: from the first Monday in October till June or later. A special term is occasionally held in the summer to hear an urgent case of national importance

treaty-making power—the President's power to make treaties with the advice and consent of the Senate. Congress may pass necessary and proper laws for carrying out the terms of a treaty, as by protecting birds that migrate between the United States and Canada. Without a treaty, it couldn't; the birds are not in interstate commerce

trial court—a court where cases are tried; not an appellate court, which reviews cases already tried

trial examiner—an officer, corresponding to a judge, who presides at administrative agency hearings; a hearing officer

unconstitutional—not in agreement with the Constitution, and hence of no effect

United States Reports—the published volumes of Supreme Court opinions, as prepared by the reporter of decisions

uphold—to find a law valid

war power—the combined powers of Congress and the President to wage war effectively. It is supported by several constitutional provisions, but would exist anyway, according to the Supreme Court, as part of the power over foreign affairs that passed to the United States upon declaring its independence. The war power, though vast, is not unlimited, the Court having held that "the Constitution of the United States is a law for rulers and people, equally in war and peace."

Justices of the Supreme Court

(Chief Justices in Italics)

Name	Appointed From	Served	Name	Appointed From	Served
John Jay	N. Y.	1789-1795	Gabriel Duval	Md.	1811-1835
John Rutledge	S. C.	1789-1791	Smith Thompson	N. Y.	1823-1843
William Cushing	Mass.	1789-1810	Robert Trimble	Ky.	1826-1828
James Wilson	Pa.	1789-1798	John McLean	Ohio	1829-1861
John Blair	Va.	1789-1796	Henry Baldwin	Pa.	1830-1844
James Iredell	N. C.	1790-1799	James M. Wayne	Ga.	1835-1867
Thomas Johnson	Md.	1791-1793	*Roger B. Taney*	Md.	1836-1864
William Paterson	N. J.	1793-1806	Philip P. Barbour	Va.	1836-1841
* *John Rutledge*	S. C.	1795-1795	John Catron	Tenn.	1837-1865
Samuel Chase	Md.	1796-1811	John McKinley	Ala.	1837-1852
Oliver Ellsworth	Conn.	1796-1800	Peter V. Daniel	Va.	1841-1860
Bushrod Washington	Va.	1798-1829	Samuel Nelson	N. Y.	1845-1872
Alfred Moore	N. C.	1799-1804	Levi Woodbury	N. H.	1845-1851
John Marshall	Va.	1801-1835	Robert C. Grier	Pa.	1846-1870
William Johnson	S. C.	1804-1834	Benjamin R. Curtis	Mass.	1851-1857
Brockholst Livingston	N. Y.	1806-1823	John A. Campbell	Ala.	1853-1861
Thomas Todd	Ky.	1807-1826	Nathan Clifford	Maine	1858-1881
Joseph Story	Mass.	1811-1845	Noah H. Swayne	Ohio	1862-1881
			Samuel F. Miller	Iowa	1862-1890
			David Davis	Ill.	1862-1877

Name	Appointed From	Served
Stephen J. Field	Calif.	1863-1897
Salmon P. Chase	Ohio	1864-1873
William Strong	Pa.	1870-1880
Joseph P. Bradley	N. J.	1870-1892
Ward Hunt	N. Y.	1873-1882
Morrison R. Waite	Ohio	1874-1888
John M. Harlan	Ky.	1877-1911
William B. Woods	Ga.	1881-1887
Stanley Matthews	Ohio	1881-1889
Horace Gray	Mass.	1882-1902
Samuel Blatchford	N. Y.	1882-1893
Lucius Q. C. Lamar	Miss.	1888-1893
Melville W. Fuller	Ill.	1888-1910
David J. Brewer	Kan.	1890-1910
Henry B. Brown	Mich.	1891-1906
George Shiras, Jr.	Pa.	1892-1903
Howell E. Jackson	Tenn.	1893-1895
Edward D. White	La.	1894-1910
Rufus W. Peckham	N. Y.	1896-1909
Joseph McKenna	Calif.	1898-1925
Oliver Wendell Holmes	Mass.	1902-1932
William R. Day	Ohio	1903-1922
William H. Moody	Mass.	1906-1910
Horace H. Lurton	Tenn.	1910-1914
Edward D. White	La.	1910-1921
Charles Evans Hughes	N. Y.	1910-1916
Willis Van Devanter	Wyo.	1911-1937
Joseph R. Lamar	Ga.	1911-1916
Mahlon Pitney	N. J.	1912-1922
James C. McReynolds	Tenn.	1914-1941

Name	Appointed From	Served
Louis D. Brandeis	Mass.	1916-1939
John H. Clarke	Ohio	1916-1922
William Howard Taft	Conn.	1921-1930
George Sutherland	Utah	1922-1938
Pierce Butler	Minn.	1923-1939
Edward T. Sanford	Tenn.	1923-1930
Harlan F. Stone	N. Y.	1925-1941
Charles Evans Hughes	N. Y.	1930-1941
Owen J. Roberts	Penn.	1930-1945
Benjamin N. Cardozo	N. Y.	1932-1938
Hugo L. Black	Ala.	1937-
Stanley F. Reed	Ky.	1938-1957
Felix Frankfurter	Mass.	1939-
William O. Douglas	Conn.	1939-
Frank Murphy	Mich.	1940-1949
Harlan F. Stone	N. Y.	1941-1946
James F. Byrnes	S. C.	1941-1942
Robert H. Jackson	N. Y.	1941-1954
Wiley B. Rutledge	Iowa	1943-1949
Harold H. Burton	Ohio	1945-1958
Fred M. Vinson	Ky.	1946-1953
Tom C. Clark	Tex.	1949-
Sherman Minton	Ind.	1949-1956
Earl Warren	Calif.	1953-
John M. Harlan	N.Y.	1955-
William J. Brennan, Jr.	N.J.	1956-
Charles E. Whittaker	Mo.	1957-
Potter Stewart	Ohio	1958-

*Recess appointment; presided over August term, but later rejected by Senate

Index

Harold Coy has been a newspaper reporter and a radio newswriter, and has always been deeply interested in American history. Born in California, Mr. Coy now lives in South Norwalk, Connecticut, where he does free lance writing. Among his books are *The First Book of Presidents; The First Book of Congress; The Americans;* and *Doctors and What They Do.*

FIRST BOOKS
classified by subject
Some titles are listed in more than one category

The ARTS

Architecture
Ballet
Bells
Color
Drawing

Gardening
How to Fix It
Jazz
Music
Paintings
Photography

Poetry
Puppets
Rhythms
Stage Costume and
   Make-Up

COMMUNICATIONS

Atlas
Codes and Ciphers
Language & How To
   Use It

Letter Writing
Maps and Globes
Measurement
Printing

Public Libraries
Teaching Machines
Television
Words

SCIENCE

Air
Airplanes
Antarctic
Archaeology
Architecture
Astronomy
Automobiles
Bees
Bells
Birds
Bridges
Bugs
Caves
Color
Conservation
Cotton
Earth

Electricity
Food
Glaciers
Glass
Human Senses
Light
Machines
Mammals
Maps and Globes
Measurement
Microbes
Mining
Ocean
Photography
Plants
Prehistoric Animals
Rhythms

Roads
Science Experiments
Sea Shells
Snakes
Sound
Space Travel
Stone Age Man
Stones
Submarines
Television
Tools
Trains
Trees
Tropical Mammals
Water
Weather
Wild Flowers

SPORTS & HOBBIES

Baseball
Basketball
Boys' Cooking
Cartoons for Kids
Cats
Chess
Christmas Joy
Codes and Ciphers

Dogs
Dolls
Football
Gardening
Horses
How to Fix It
Jokes
Magic

Photography
Physical Fitness
Sailing
Stones
Surprising Facts
Swimming

SOCIAL STUDIES
United States

Atlas
American History
American Revolution
California Gold Rush
The China Clippers
Civil War Land Battles
Civil War Naval Actions
Congress
Constitution
Early Settlers

Hawaii
Holidays
Indian Wars
Indians
National Monuments
National Parks
Negroes
New England
New World Explorers

Oregon Trail
Panama Canal
Pioneers
Presidents
Supreme Court
United Nations
War of 1812
Washington, D.C.
World War I
World War II

The World About Us

Africa
Ancient Bible Lands
Ancient Egypt
Ancient Mesopotamia
   and Persia
Ancient Greece
Ancient Rome
Antarctic
Archaeology
Australia
Barbarian Invaders
Brazil
Canada

Communist China
Congo
England
Eskimos
Festivals
France
Ghana
India
Israel
Italy
Japan
Kings
Medieval Man
Mediterranean

Mexico
Netherlands
New Zealand
Ocean
Pakistan
South America
Soviet Union
United Nations
Vikings
West Germany
West Indies
World War I
World War II

People and Products

Conservation
Cotton
Cowboys

Firemen
Food
Glass

Nurses
Supermarkets
Water

LITERATURE &
LANGUAGE ARTS

Codes and Ciphers
Color
Fairy Tales
Language & How To
   Use It

Letter Writing
Legendary Beings
Maps and Globes
Mythology
Mythical Beasts

Norse Legends
Poetry
Printing
Teaching Machines
Words

TRANSPORTATION

Airplanes
Automobiles
Boats
Bridges

Maps and Globes
Panama Canal
Roads
Ships

Space Travel
Trains
Water